SPACE FACTS AND FIGURES

GALAXIES AND STARS

Nancy Dickmann

WINDMILL BOOKS

Published in 2019 by **Windmill Books**, an imprint of Rosen Publishing
29 East 21st Street, New York, NY 10010

For Brown Bear Books Ltd:
Text and Editor: Nancy Dickmann
Children's Publisher: Anne O'Daly
Editorial Director: Lindsey Lowe
Design Manager: Keith Davis
Designer and Illustrator: Supriya Sahai
Picture Manager: Sophie Mortimer

Concept development: Square and Circus/Brown Bear Books Ltd

Picture Credits:
Front cover: Supriya Sahai
iStock: adventtr 6, John Camemolla 14, NASA: ESA/G. Illingworth/D. Magee/P. Oesch,
University of California, Santa Cruz/R. Bouwens, Leiden University/HUDF09 Team 19, ESA/
Hubble Legacy Archive 20r, Ibata (Strasboug Observatory,ULP), R/2MASS 26, JPL-Caltech 8, 23,
24, 25, 27, 29, JPL-Caltech/UCLA 20l; Shutterstock: Aphelleon 7, 28; Denis Belitsky 4–5, Marcel
Clemens 4, Egyptian Studio 9, Yongyut Kumsri 22, NASA Images 21, olegganko 16, Outer Space
12–13, Jurik Peter 14–15, Triff 18, vcal 16–17; Wikipedia: NASA/ESA/The Hubble Heritage Team
(STScI/AURA)/J. Blakeslee (Washington State University) 20c

Key: t=top, b=bottom, c=center, l=left, r=right

Brown Bear Books has made every attempt to contact the copyright holder.
If anyone has any information please contact licensing@brownbearbooks.co.uk

Cataloging-in-Publication Data

Names: Dickmann, Nancy.
Title: Galaxies and stars / Nancy Dickmann.
Description: New York : Windmill Books, 2019. | Series: Space facts and figures |
Includes glossary and index.
Identifiers: LCCN ISBN 9781508195153 (pbk.) | ISBN 9781508195146 (library bound) |
ISBN 9781508195160 (6 pack)
Subjects: LCSH: Stars--Juvenile literature. | Galaxies--Juvenile literature. |
Astronomy--Juvenile literature.
Classification: LCC QB801.7 D53 2019 | DDC 523.8--dc23

Manufactured in the United States of America

CPSIA Compliance Information: Batch #BS18WM:
For Further Information contact Rosen Publishing, New York, New York at 1-800-237-9932

CONTENTS

WHAT'S OUT THERE?

Look up at the night sky and you might see hundreds or even thousands of stars. Space is a huge place!

We live on **planet** Earth. It **orbits** a **star** that we call the sun. The sun, planets, and other space objects make up the **solar system**. The sun is part of a **galaxy** called the Milky Way. This is a giant spiral-shaped group of stars. The Milky Way is just one of the countless galaxies in the **universe**.

The Hubble Space **Telescope** studies stars and galaxies from space.

Gravity is the force that holds galaxies together.

Some pairs of stars orbit each other.

GO FIGURE!

Planets in the solar system: 8
Stars in the solar system: 1
Stars in the Milky Way: at least 100 billion
Galaxies in the universe: at least 2 trillion

The Milky Way

All the stars you can see in the night sky are part of the Milky Way.

Many of the other stars in the universe also have planets around them.

WHAT IS A STAR?

Long ago, many people thought that stars were lights. They thought the lights attached to a huge dome over the Earth. The truth is much more impressive.

Stars are giant balls of glowing gas. They are incredibly hot. Deep inside a star, a process called **nuclear fusion** produces **energy**. Stars give off this energy in the form of heat and light. It can take up to a million years for energy from the center of a star to make it all the way out to its outer layers.

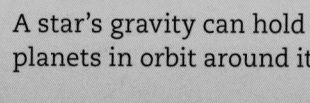

A star's gravity can hold planets in orbit around it.

Stars are made of layers, one inside the other.

All life on Earth depends on heat and light from the sun.

Core

Radiative zone

Convection zone

Photosphere

GO FIGURE!

Temperature in the sun's core (center):
27 million °F (15 million °C)
Temperature at the sun's surface:
10,000 °F (5,538 °C)
Diameter of the sun: 864,000 miles
(1,390,473 kilometers)
Age of the sun: 4.6 billion years
What the sun is made of: 92% hydrogen,
8% helium

It took a long time for people to realize that the sun was like other stars.

Stars are mostly made of **hydrogen** and **helium**.

HOW STARS FORM

When the universe began, trillions of stars formed in a short time. New stars are still being made today.

Stars form inside giant clouds of dust and gas, called **nebulas**. Inside a nebula, gravity makes gas and dust collapse together. The bigger these clumps get, the more gravity they have. They attract even more material, growing bigger and more **dense**. Eventually the new star gets massive enough for nuclear fusion to start. It begins to shine.

In its early stages, a star is called a protostar. The bright red spots in this nebula are protostars.

Some of the dust in a nebula can form planets and **asteroids**.

GO FIGURE!

Star formation time (for a star similar to the sun): 50 million years
Average surface temperature of a small star: 5,000–7,000 °F (2,760–3,870 °C)
Average surface temperature of an enormous star: 53,500 °F (29,700 °C)

A star's **core** needs to reach 27 million °F (15 million °C) before it can shine.

Gas and dust clouds in the Eagle nebula

Small groups of "sister stars" often form together inside a nebula.

New stars are no longer forming as often as before.

TYPES OF STARS

All stars are giant balls of hot, glowing gas, but they come in different sizes and colors.

Most stars are grouped by size and temperature. The smallest, coolest stars are called red dwarfs. They are very dim and hard to see from Earth. They burn their hydrogen fuel slowly, so they last a long time. The biggest, hottest stars are blue and very bright. They burn through their hydrogen fuel in just a few million years. That's fast for a star!

From coolest to hottest, star colors are red, orange, yellow, white, and blue.

COOLEST   HOTTEST

GO FIGURE!

Minimum size of a star: 80 times as much **mass** as Jupiter
Largest stars: about 250 times as much mass as the sun
Yellow dwarfs: about 8% of all stars
Brightest stars: more than 30,000 times as bright as the sun

More than three-quarters of all stars are red dwarfs.

The blue star Zeta Ophiuchi is about 8.5 times wider than the sun.

Astronomers think that red dwarfs can shine for trillions of years.

The sun is a medium-sized star called a yellow dwarf.

The sun only appears brighter than other stars because it is so close.

SUPERNOVA!

Stars do not shine forever. When they run out of fuel, they "die." Sometimes this happens in a very spectacular way.

The way that a star "dies" depends on how massive it is. All stars turn into red giants when they begin to run out of fuel. They swell up, becoming cooler and dimmer. A fairly small star, like the sun, will then collapse to form a dense white star called a white dwarf. A much bigger star will explode in an event called **supernova**.

When the sun becomes a red giant, it will be big enough to swallow up Mercury, Venus, and Earth.

After a supernova, a glowing cloud of gas is left behind.

A white dwarf is about the size of Earth, but has as much mass as the sun.

GO FIGURE!

Supernova size: a star must have at least 10 times as much mass as the sun
Supernova temperature: more than 100 billion degrees
White dwarf size: no more than 1.4 times as much mass as the sun
White dwarf surface gravity: 100,000 times as strong as Earth's gravity

The material left over after a supernova can form a **black hole**.

When a white dwarf runs out of energy, it will stop shining and become a black dwarf.

PULSARS

The super-dense leftovers of a supernova explosion form something called a neutron star. Some of these neutron stars turn into pulsars.

Pulsars are small—about the size of a city. But they are very dense. Pulsars spin in space. They send out two narrow beams of bright light. The beams go in opposite directions. They sweep across the sky, like the light of a lighthouse. From Earth, it looks like they are blinking on and off.

The Parkes radio telescope in Australia has found many pulsars.

After many years, a pulsar will eventually slow down and stop sending out light.

Pulsars spin around much faster than stars or planets do.

Pulsars were discovered in 1967 by Jocelyn Bell Burnell.

Radiation beam

GO FIGURE!

Pulsars discovered so far: more than 2,300

Pulsar rotation: from 1 to 700 times per second

Average pulsar size: from 12.4 to 14.9 miles (20 to 24 kilometers) in diameter

Average surface temperature: 1.8 million °F (1 million °C)

A piece of neutron star the size of a sugar cube would weigh as much as Mount Everest.

CONSTELLATIONS

When we look up at the night sky, it seems like the stars form patterns or pictures. Some of these are called constellations.

Since ancient times, people have given names to star patterns. They looked for patterns that looked like creatures or characters from stories and legends. Astronomers have now agreed on 88 official **constellations**. Even though they look close together, the stars in a constellation are not necessarily near each other in space.

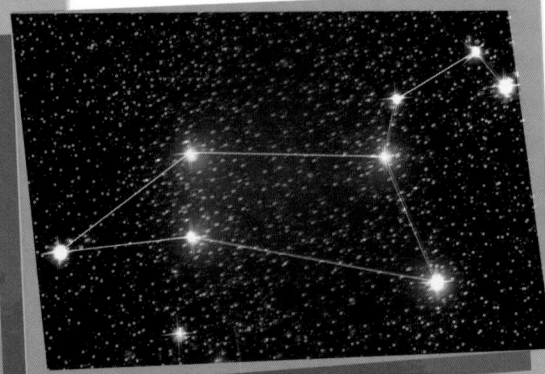

The constellations of the zodiac, including Leo, form a ring around the sun.

People used to use constellations to find their way.

The constellation Orion is named after a hunter in Greek mythology.

Patterns that didn't make the list of official constellations are called **asterisms**.

The Big Dipper is an asterism. It forms part of a constellation called Ursa Major.

GO FIGURE!

Constellations in the zodiac: 13 (not 12 as most people assume)
Largest constellation: Hydra (covers about 3% of the sky)
Smallest constellation: Crux (covers less than 0.2% of the sky)

The constellations you see depend on your location and the time of year.

GALAXIES

Most stars are grouped together in galaxies. Galaxies come in different shapes, but they are all enormous.

Scientists think there may be 100 billion galaxies in the universe. Each of these galaxies contains hundreds of thousands or even billions of stars. Galaxies do not stay still. Instead, they move through space. The universe is constantly expanding. This makes galaxies move away from each other.

Galaxies also contain planets, moons, and clouds of dust.

The Hubble Space Telescope produced this image, showing 10,000 galaxies in a small area of space.

Many galaxies are part of larger groups and clusters.

The space in between galaxies is very empty.

GO FIGURE!

Closest large galaxy to Earth:
Andromeda, 2.5 million **light-years** away
Farthest galaxy discovered: GN-z11,
32 billion light-years away

Some stars are not part of a galaxy. Scientists call them "stellar outcasts."

GALAXY SHAPES

Galaxies come in different shapes. Scientists put them into groups based on their shape.

More than half of all galaxies have a spiral shape. The stars form huge "arms" that spiral out from the center. Some spiral galaxies have a group of stars shaped like a flat bar stretching across the center. They are called barred spirals. Other galaxies are smooth and oval-shaped. They are called elliptical galaxies. Lenticular galaxies have a shape halfway between spiral and elliptical.

Spiral

Elliptical

Lenticular

A few galaxies have unusual shapes like toothpicks or rings.

Galaxies sometimes collide with each other.

A barred spiral galaxy

Elliptical galaxies often have stars that are older than in spiral galaxies.

The stars in a galaxy rotate around the galaxy's center.

THE MILKY WAY

On a clear, very dark night, you might see a fuzzy white band of stars stretching across the sky. It's our galaxy!

All of the stars that you see in the sky are part of our galaxy, the Milky Way. It contains billions of stars arranged in a spiral shape, with a bar across the center. This makes the Milky Way a barred spiral galaxy. The spiral is flat, like a disc. We see the rest of the galaxy edge-on. This is why it looks like a line across the sky.

The word "galaxy" comes from the Greek word for "milk."

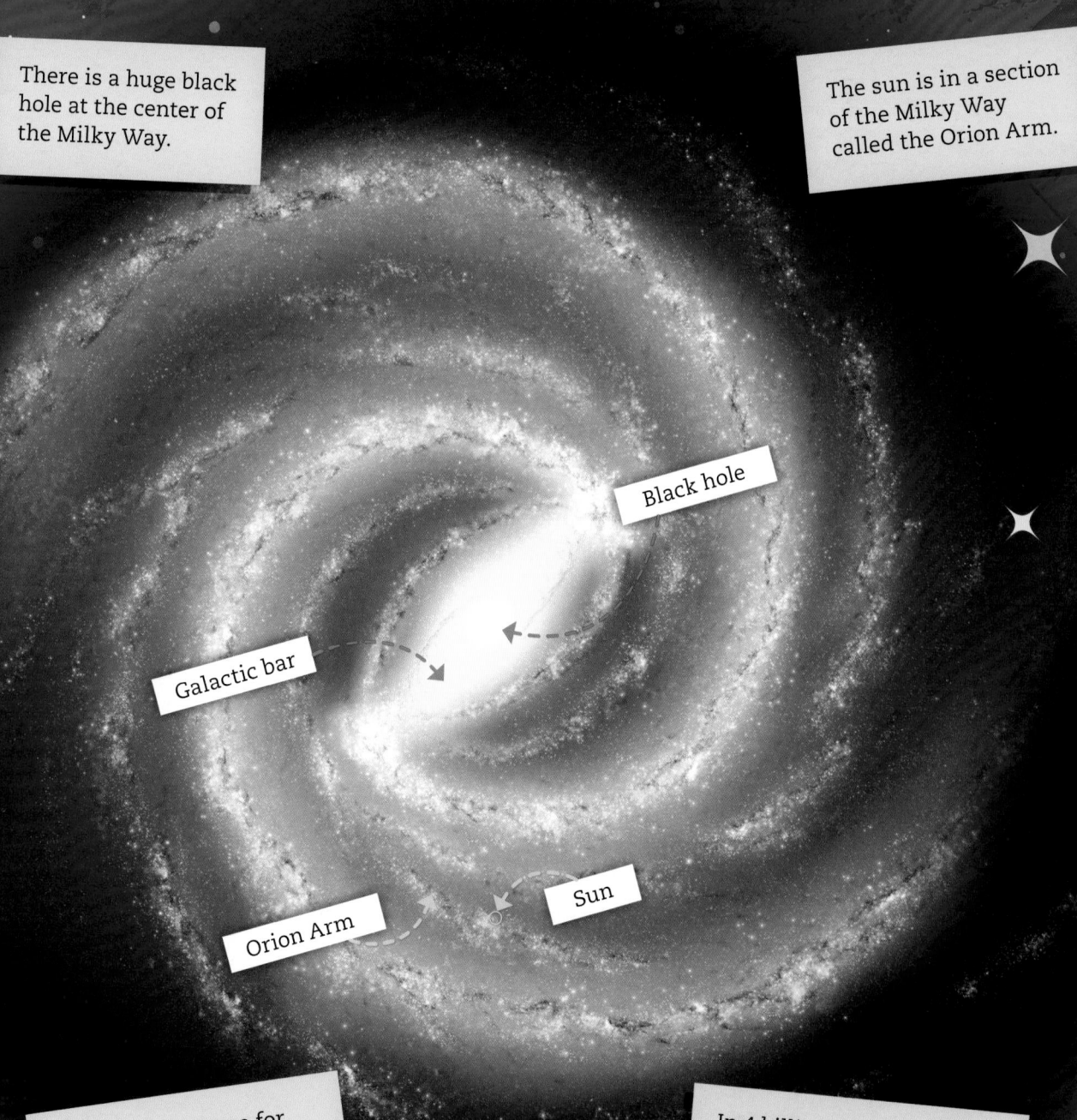

There is a huge black hole at the center of the Milky Way.

The sun is in a section of the Milky Way called the Orion Arm.

Black hole

Galactic bar

Orion Arm

Sun

The Chinese name for the Milky Way translates to "silver river."

In 4 billion years, the Milky Way will collide with the Andromeda galaxy.

BLACK HOLES

A black hole is not empty. It has a huge amount of mass, which means that its gravity is very strong.

A black hole's gravitational force is so strong that nothing can escape it, not even light. Because no light can escape, we can't see black holes directly. Instead, astronomers look for other clues. Gas might heat up and glow as it falls into a black hole. The black hole's gravity may affect nearby stars.

Material may form a disk around the black hole as it is pulled in.

GO FIGURE!

Medium-sized black hole: 10 miles (16 kilometers) in diameter
Mass of Sagittarius A: equal to 4 million suns
Diameter of Sagittarius A: probably about 850,000 miles (1.37 million kilometers)

Scientists think that most galaxies have an enormous black hole at the center.

The black hole at the center of the Milky Way is called Sagittarius A.

A medium-sized black hole may only be a few miles across but have as much mass as a large star.

The sun does not have enough mass to ever turn into a black hole.

GALACTIC NEIGHBORS

There are nearby galaxies that are like "neighbors" in space. Even so, they are way too far away ever to visit!

The Milky Way is part of a small group of galaxies called the Local Group. Some of these galaxies are small and are called "dwarf galaxies." Our closest neighbor is a dwarf galaxy called Canis Major. The nearest large galaxy is a spiral galaxy called Andromeda. It can be seen in the sky as a faint fuzzy blob.

Canis Major

Sun

Milky Way

The Milky Way's gravity is slowly pulling Canis Major apart.

The Local Group is part of a larger family of galaxies called the Virgo Supercluster.

The Canis Major dwarf galaxy was discovered in 2003.

Andromeda, our closest large galaxy

The Large and Small Magellanic Clouds are dwarf galaxies near the Milky Way.

At current speeds, it would take a spacecraft about 750 million years to reach Canis Major.

GO FIGURE!

Galaxies in the Local Group: at least 54 (includes dwarf galaxies)
Distance to Canis Major: 25,000 light-years, or 147,000,000,000,000,000 miles (236,000,000,000,000,000 kilometers)
Distance to the Large Magellanic Cloud: 179,000 light-years
Distance to the Small Magellanic Cloud: 210,000 light-years

QUIZ

Try this quiz and test your knowledge of stars and galaxies! The answers are on page 32.

1 What holds galaxies together?
A. glue
B. gravity
C. nebulas

2 What are stars made of?
A. hydrogen and helium
B. oxygen and carbon dioxide
C. fire and water

3 What happens inside a star's core?
A. a really hot party
B. planets and comets form
C. nuclear fusion

4 Which type of star is the sun?
A. blue supergiant
B. yellow dwarf
C. pink troll

5 What is it called when a star explodes?
A. a supercluster
B. a supermarket
C. a supernova

6 What is a constellation?
A. a group of stars that form a pattern
B. a place where new stars form
C. an argument between two aliens

7 What shape of galaxy is the Milky Way?
A. heart-shaped
B. barred spiral
C. elliptical

8 Why can't light escape from a black hole?
A. it's too dark
B. a black hole's gravity is too strong
C. the light has no sense of direction

GLOSSARY

asterism a pattern of stars in the sky that is not an official constellation

asteroid a large chunk of rock left over from when the planets formed

astronomer person who studies the sun, the planets, and other objects in space

black hole object that has so much mass that nothing can escape its gravity, not even light

constellation a group of stars that appear to form a pattern or picture when seen from Earth

core the center of a star, planet, moon, or other object

dense having a lot of matter in a small space

energy the ability to do work

galaxy collection of billions of stars held together by gravity

gravity a force that pulls objects together. The heavier or closer an object is, the stronger its gravity, or pull.

helium very light gas that is produced in a star's core

hydrogen light gas that can fuse into helium inside a star

light-year the distance that light travels in one year

mass the measure of the amount of material in an object

nebula cloud of dust or gas in space

nuclear fusion reaction in which two or more atoms fuse together, which releases energy

orbit the path an object takes around a larger object; or, to take such a path

planet large, round object that orbits a star

solar system a group of planets that circles a star

star large, hot ball of glowing gas

supernova the explosion that takes place when a very large star runs out of fuel and collapses

telescope tool used for studying space, which gathers information about things that are far away

universe everything that exists, including all matter and energy

FURTHER RESOURCES

Books

Aguilar, David A. *Super Stars: The Biggest, Hottest, Brightest, and Most Explosive Stars in the Milky Way.* National Geographic Children's Books, 2010.

Ford, Adam. *Stars: A Family Guide to the Night Sky (Discover Together Guides).* Roost Books, 2016.

Gifford, Clive. *Stars, Galaxies and the Milky Way (Watch This Space).* Wayland, 2015.

Kopp, Megan. *The Milky Way and Other Galaxies (The Solar System and Beyond).* Capstone Press, 2011.

Prinja, Raman. *Night Sky Watcher: Your Guide to the Stars and Planets (Watcher Guides).* QEB Publishing, 2016.

Websites

For web resources related
to the subject of this book, go to:
www.windmillbooks.com/weblinks
and select this book's title.

INDEX

Answers to quiz:
1. b; 2. a; 3. c; 4. b; 5. c; 6. a; 7. b; 8. b